GCSE English Literature AQA Anthology

Relationships

The Workbook
Higher Level

This book will help you prepare for the Anthology part of your GCSE English Literature exam.

It contains lots of questions designed to make you an expert on writing about poetry.

It's ideal for use as a homework book or to help you revise.

What CGP is all about

Our sole aim here at CGP is to produce the highest quality books — carefully written, immaculately presented and dangerously close to being funny.

Then we work our socks off to get them out to you — at the cheapest possible prices.

Contents

How to Use this Book... 1

Section One — Poems from the Literary Heritage

Sonnet 116 — William Shakespeare 4
To His Coy Mistress — Andrew Marvell 6
The Farmer's Bride — Charlotte Mew 8
Sonnet 43 — Elizabeth Barrett Browning 10
Sister Maude — Christina Rossetti 12
Nettles — Vernon Scannell 14
Born Yesterday — Philip Larkin 16

Section Two — Contemporary Poems

The Manhunt — Simon Armitage 18
Hour — Carol Ann Duffy 20
In Paris With You — James Fenton 22
Quickdraw — Carol Ann Duffy 24
Ghazal — Mimi Khalvati 26
Brothers — Andrew Forster 28
Praise Song For My Mother — Grace Nichols 30
Harmonium — Simon Armitage 32

Section Three — Themes

Relationships 34
Negative Emotions 36
Love 37
Time 38
Getting Older 39
Death 40
Memory 41
Nature 42
Pain and Desire 43

Section Four — Analysing Answers

Mark Scheme 44
Adding Quotes and Developing Points 45
Marking Answer Extracts 47
Marking a Complete Answer 50

Acknowledgements 52

Published by Coordination Group Publications Ltd.

Editors:
Rachael Powers, Edward Robinson, Hayley Thompson

Produced with:
Alison Smith, Peter Thomas, Nicola Woodfin

Contributors:
Caroline Bagshaw, Alison Smith

With thanks to Glenn Rogers and Emma Willshaw for the proofreading
and Jan Greenway for the copyright research.

ISBN: 978 1 84762 532 8
Groovy website: www.cgpbooks.co.uk
Jolly bits of clipart from CorelDRAW®
Printed by Elanders Hindson Ltd, Newcastle upon Tyne

Based on the classic CGP style created by Richard Parsons.

Photocopying — it's dull, it takes ages... and sometimes it's a bit naughty.
Luckily, it's dead cheap, easy and quick to order more copies of this book
from CGP — just call us on 0870 750 1242. Phew!

Text, design, layout and original illustrations © Coordination Group Publications Ltd. 2010
All rights reserved.

How to Use this Book

This book is for anyone studying the Relationships cluster of the AQA GCSE English Literature Poetry Anthology. It's got loads of questions in it to help you get your head around the poems.

Sections One and Two are About the Poems

There's a double page on each poem. It looks a bit like this:

There's some info about the poet here.

There's plenty of space around the poem for you to make notes.

Difficult words are defined in the Poem Dictionary.

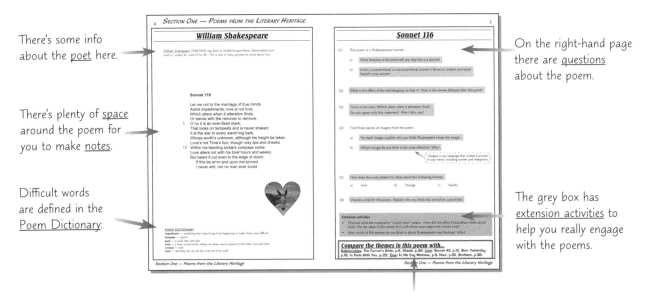

On the right-hand page there are questions about the poem.

The grey box has extension activities to help you really engage with the poems.

The top tip box lists some of the other poems in the cluster with similar themes.

A little bit about the questions...

This is the most important bit...

1) The questions are designed to get you thinking for yourself about the poem.
2) They start off nice and simple, then get trickier as you go down the page.
3) Answer the questions as thoroughly as you can.
   It's important to get to know the poems inside out.
4) Answers can be found in the separate Answer Book.

The questions in these two sections mostly ask you about technical stuff like language, structure and form.

How to Use this Book

Comparing the poems is one of the most important things you'll have to do — that's what Section Three is all about. The questions in it will help you link the different poems by their themes.

Section Three is About the Themes

A double-page spread in the Themes section looks a bit like this:

A different theme is covered on each page.

There are questions about the theme and how different poems relate to it.

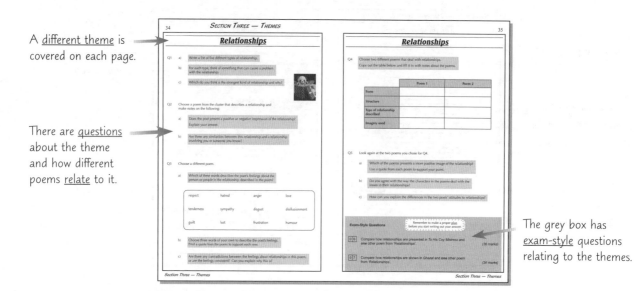

The grey box has exam-style questions relating to the themes.

This is a Really Useful Section

1) The questions are designed to get you thinking about the poems' themes and ideas.

2) They'll also get you to compare the poems — which is just what you'll need to do to get good marks in your exam.

3) The exam-style questions are exactly that — questions like the ones you'll get in your exam. Use them to practise planning and writing answers. Trust me, it'll really help when it comes to the real thing.

> Remember: the themes covered in this section aren't the only ones you can write about — they're here to give you some ideas. Once you start thinking about the poems and comparing them with each other, you're bound to come up with a few more of your own.

How to Use this Book

How to Use this Book

One of the best ways to learn what gets you marks is to analyse some exam-style answers. So that's what you'll be doing in Section Four. You lucky thing, you.

Section Four lets you Analyse some Answers

A page in Section Four looks a bit like this:

These instructions tell you what you have to do (more on this below).

This is a sample extract from a student's answer.

There's an exam-style question at the top of the page.

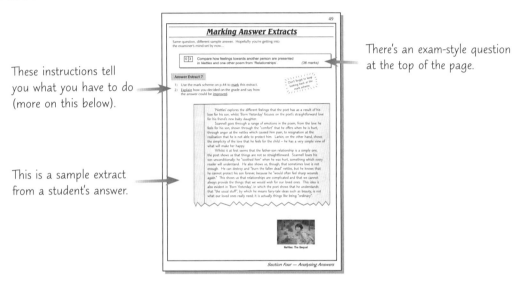

This Section Helps You Understand How to Do Well

1) Most of the questions in this section ask you to grade a sample exam answer.

2) They'll also ask you to say what the answer needs to do to score more marks — this will help you understand how to improve your own answers.

3) Some of the questions ask you to extend a point or give a quote from the poem to back a point up. This helps you to understand how to really use the poems to write a top-notch answer.

Remember: there's more than one right answer to the questions that you'll get in your poetry exam. These sample answers are just designed to show you the kinds of points you'll need to make and the kind of writing style you'll need to use to get a top grade.

How to Use this Book

William Shakespeare

William Shakespeare (1564-1616) was born in Stratford-upon-Avon, Warwickshire, but lived in London for most of his life. This is one of many sonnets he wrote about love.

Sonnet 116

Let me not to the marriage of true minds
Admit impediments; love is not love
Which alters when it alteration finds,
Or bends with the remover to remove.
5   O no it is an ever-fixed mark,
That looks on tempests and is never shaken;
It is the star to every wand'ring bark,
Whose worth's unknown, although his height be taken.
Love's not Time's fool, though rosy lips and cheeks
10   Within his bending sickle's compass come:
Love alters not with his brief hours and weeks,
But bears it out even to the edge of doom.
    If this be error and upon me proved,
    I never writ, nor no man ever loved.

POEM DICTIONARY
impediment — something that stops things from happening or makes them more difficult
tempests — storms
bark — a small ship with sails
sickle — a sharp, curved tool for cutting corn always used on pictures of Old Father Time and Death
compass — reach
doom — doomsday: the very last day at the end of the world

Section One — Poems from the Literary Heritage

Sonnet 116

Q1 This poem is a Shakespearean sonnet.

   a) What features of the poem tell you that this is a sonnet?

   b) Is this a conventional or unconventional sonnet in terms of content and style? Explain your answer.

Q2 What is the effect of the end-stopping on line 4? How is the sonnet different after this point?

Q3 "Love is not love / Which alters when it alteration finds".
    Do you agree with this statement? Why / Why not?

Q4 Find three pieces of imagery from the poem.

   a) For each image, explain why you think Shakespeare chose this image.

   b) Which image do you think is the most effective? Why?

   Imagery is any language that creates a picture in your mind, including similes and metaphors.

Q5 How does the poet present his ideas about the following themes:

   a) time   b) change   c) loyalty

Q6 Choose a title for this poem. Explain why you think this would be a good title.

Extension activities
- Find out what the expression "courtly love" means. How did this affect Elizabethan ideas about love? Do the ideas in this poem fit in with those associated with courtly love?
- How much of this sonnet do you think is about Shakespeare's real feelings? Why?

Compare the themes in this poem with...
Relationships: The Farmer's Bride, p.8, Ghazal, p.26; Love: Sonnet 43, p.10, Born Yesterday, p.16; In Paris With You, p.22; Time: To His Coy Mistress, p.6, Hour, p.20, Brothers, p.28.

Section One — Poems from the Literary Heritage

Andrew Marvell

Andrew Marvell (1621-1678) was born in Yorkshire and raised in Hull. After studying at Cambridge, he travelled in Europe, before taking a post as a tutor. He's known as a metaphysical poet, as he wrote about philosophical subjects like life and soul.

To His Coy Mistress

Had we but world enough, and time,
This coyness, Lady, were no crime,
We would sit down and think which way
To walk and pass our long love's day.
5 Thou by the Indian Ganges' side
Shouldst rubies find; I by the tide
Of Humber would complain. I would
Love you ten years before the Flood,
And you should, if you please, refuse
10 Till the conversion of the Jews.
My vegetable love should grow
Vaster than empires, and more slow;
An hundred years should go to praise
Thine eyes, and on thy forehead gaze;
15 Two hundred to adore each breast;
But thirty thousand to the rest;
An age at least to every part,
And the last age should show your heart.
For, Lady, you deserve this state,
20 Nor would I love at lower rate.

But at my back I always hear
Time's wingèd chariot hurrying near;
And yonder all before us lie
Deserts of vast eternity.
25 Thy beauty shall no more be found,
Nor, in thy marble vault, shall sound
My echoing song; then worms shall try
That long preserved virginity,
And your quaint honour turn to dust,
30 And into ashes all my lust.
The grave's a fine and private place,
But none, I think, do there embrace.

Now therefore, while the youthful hue
Sits on thy skin like morning dew,
35 And while thy willing soul transpires
At every pore with instant fires,
Now let us sport us while we may,
And now, like amorous birds of prey,
Rather at once our time devour
40 Than languish in his slow-chapt power.
Let us roll all our strength and all
Our sweetness up into one ball,
And tear our pleasures with rough strife
Through the iron gates of life.
45 Thus, though we cannot make our sun
Stand still, yet we will make him run.

Oops, there goes my quaint honour...

POEM DICTIONARY
coy — shy
mistress — a man's long-term companion/sweetheart
quaint — too prim and proper or old-fashioned
slow-chapt — slow-jawed, i.e. chewing slowly

Section One — Poems from the Literary Heritage

To His Coy Mistress

Q1   a)   Name a poetic feature that Marvell uses in this poem.

     b)   Do you think this feature successfully supports what Marvell is trying to say? Explain your answer.

Q2   Marvell wants his mistress to make her mind up quickly. Find a quote that makes this clear.

Q3   In the poem the poet refers to two rivers — the Humber and the Ganges.

     a)   Copy the table below and list the ideas that you think the poet is trying to associate with each river.

Ganges	Humber
Inaccessible	

We've put one here to start you off.

     b)   What is the effect of the contrast between the two rivers?

Q4   What evidence can you find in the poem for the importance of time to the poet?

Q5   Why do you think the poet uses the image of the "marble vault" in line 26?

Q6   Write a short paragraph explaining in your own words what the poet is trying to say in the last two lines of the poem.

Extension activity

- "Coy" is quite an old-fashioned adjective. Can you think of a title that would be better for explaining the poem's theme to a 21st century audience?

This poem has similar themes to....
Relationships: In Paris With You, p.22, The Farmer's Bride, p.8; Love: Sonnet 116, p.4; Time: Hour, p.20; Death: Harmonium, p.32; Nature: Ghazal, p.26, Praise Song For My Mother, p.30.

Section One — Poems from the Literary Heritage

Charlotte Mew

Charlotte Mew (1869-1928) was born in London. Despite attracting praise for her poetry from Thomas Hardy, Virginia Woolf and Siegfried Sassoon, Mew never achieved commercial success and spent most of her life in poverty.

The Farmer's Bride

Three Summers since I chose a maid,
Too young maybe — but more's to do
At harvest-time than bide and woo.
    When us was wed she turned afraid
5 Of love and me and all things human;
Like the shut of a winter's day
Her smile went out, and 'twasn't a woman —
    More like a little frightened fay.
        One night, in the Fall, she runned away.

10 'Out 'mong the sheep, her be,' they said,
Should properly have been abed;
But sure enough she wasn't there
Lying awake with her wide brown stare.
    So over seven-acre field and up-along across the down
15 We chased her, flying like a hare
    Before our lanterns. To Church-Town
All in a shiver and a scare
We caught her, fetched her home at last
And turned the key upon her, fast.

20 She does the work about the house
As well as most, but like a mouse:
    Happy enough to chat and play
    With birds and rabbits and such as they,
    So long as men-folk keep away.
25 'Not near, not near!' her eyes beseech
When one of us comes within reach.
    The women say that beasts in stall
    Look round like children at her call.
    I've hardly heard her speak at all.

30 Shy as a leveret, swift as he,
Straight and slight as a young larch tree,
Sweet as the first wild violets, she,
To her wild self. But what to me?

The short days shorten and the oaks are brown,
35   The blue smoke rises to the low grey sky,
One leaf in the still air falls slowly down,
    A magpie's spotted feathers lie
On the black earth spread white with rime,
The berries redden up to Christmas-time.
40   What's Christmas-time without there be
    Some other in the house than we!

    She sleeps up in the attic there
        Alone, poor maid. 'Tis but a stair
    Betwixt us. Oh! my God! the down,
45 The soft young down of her; the brown,
The brown of her — her eyes, her hair, her hair!

POEM DICTIONARY
bide — wait
fay — a fairy
leveret — a young hare
rime — ice

The Farmer's Bride

Q1 'The Farmer's Bride' is a narrative poem.

How do we know this?

Q2 Make a list of any dialect words you can find in the poem. What is the effect of the dialect?

Q3 Below are three of the main feelings in 'The Farmer's Bride'. Find an example of each one in the poem.

a) fear
b) frustration
c) desire

But more's to do
At harvest time, than twit-twoo

Q4 The farmer's bride is portrayed in the poem as being both courageous and scared.

a) Find a quote from the poem which provides evidence for each of these things.

b) Do you think she is more courageous or more scared? Why?

Q5 What do you think is the importance of the Christmas image in lines 39-41?

Q6 What is your attitude towards the farmer? Do you sympathise with him or not? Back up your answer with examples from the poem.

Extension activities
- Do you think that the story will eventually end happily or not? Use the poem to support your view.
- Write a response to the farmer giving the bride's point of view. Try to write your response as a dramatic monologue.

Other poems have similar themes...
Pain and Desire: To His Coy Mistress, p.6, Quickdraw, p.24; Memory: Brothers, p.28, The Manhunt, p.18; Nature: Praise Song For My Mother, p.30; Relationships: Ghazal, p.26.

Section One — Poems from the Literary Heritage

Elizabeth Barrett Browning

<u>Elizabeth Barrett Browning</u> (1806-1861) was born into an affluent family in County Durham. A successful poet in her own right, she was influenced heavily by (and had a profound influence on) the poetry of her husband, Robert Browning.

Sonnet 43

How do I love thee? Let me count the ways! –
I love thee to the depth and breadth and height
My soul can reach, when feeling out of sight
For the ends of Being and Ideal Grace.
5   I love thee to the level of everyday's
Most quiet need, by sun and candlelight –
I love thee freely, as men strive for Right, –
I love thee purely, as they turn from Praise;
I love thee with the passion, put to use
10   In my old griefs, ... and with my childhood's faith:
I love thee with the love I seemed to lose
With my lost Saints, – I love thee with the breath,
Smiles, tears, of all my life! – and, if God choose,
I shall but love thee better after death.

Section One — Poems from the Literary Heritage

Sonnet 43

Q1 The poem opens with a question. Why do you think this is?

Q2 a) What form is the poem written in?

   b) Is this a surprising choice considering the subject of the poem?

Q3 Barrett Browning starts many lines of this poem with the same words.

   a) What is this called? Choose the correct answer from the options below.

   alliteration   assonance   anaphora

   b) What effect does it have in this poem?

Q4 Look at the image in line 6. What is the effect of this image?

Q5 Although the poet uses the word "thee" a lot, she also frequently uses "I" and "my". Do you think the poem is more focused on the poet herself or her loved one? Explain your answer.

Q6 The poem also contains many examples of religious imagery. Do you think this makes it less relevant to modern readers? Explain your answer.

Extension activities
- What type of person do you think the narrator of this poem is?
- Lots of people have this poem as a reading when they get married. Do you think it is a good choice? Explain your answer by referring to the poem.

Poems which explore similar feelings are...
Love: Sonnet 116, p.4, Ghazal, p.26; **Death:** To His Coy Mistress, p.6; **Time:** Hour, p.20; **Relationships:** The Manhunt, p.18; **Getting Older:** Praise Song For My Mother, p.30.

Section One — Poems from the Literary Heritage

Christina Rossetti

Christina Rossetti (1830-1894) was born in London. She wrote many romantic, religious and children's poems, including 'In the Bleak Midwinter', which was set to music and became one of our best-loved Christmas carols.

Sister Maude

Who told my mother of my shame,
    Who told my father of my dear?
Oh who but Maude, my sister Maude,
    Who lurked to spy and peer.

5   Cold he lies, as cold as stone,
    With his clotted curls about his face:
The comeliest corpse in all the world
    And worthy of a queen's embrace.

You might have spared his soul, sister,
10   Have spared my soul, your own soul too:
Though I had not been born at all,
    He'd never have looked at you.

My father may sleep in Paradise,
    My mother at Heaven-gate:
15 But sister Maude shall get no sleep
    Either early or late.

My father may wear a golden gown,
    My mother a crown may win;
If my dear and I knocked at Heaven-gate
20   Perhaps they'd let us in:
But sister Maude, oh sister Maude,
    Bide *you* with death and sin.

POEM DICTIONARY
comeliest — the most attractive
bide — stay

Maude had committed two sins —
spying and crimes against fashion

Section One — Poems from the Literary Heritage

Sister Maude

Q1 Write a short paragraph summarising what the narrator says in the first two stanzas of the poem.

Q2 'Sister Maude' contains many end-stopped lines. What effect do these have?

Q3 What does the narrator imply was the motive for Maude's crime? Which line from the poem supports this?

Q4 Rossetti uses alliteration to describe her lover. How effective is the alliteration in building up a picture of him?

"No, you don't understand — *I* do the spying."

Q5 In this poem, what is the effect of:

a) the religious imagery, such as "Paradise" and "Heaven-gate"?

b) the use of sibilance?

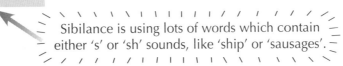

Sibilance is using lots of words which contain either 's' or 'sh' sounds, like 'ship' or 'sausages'.

Q6 Do you sympathise with the narrator of this poem? Write a paragraph explaining why or why not. Make sure you back up your answer with examples from the text.

Extension activities

- Do you think that the narrator's anger with her sister is just a silly argument or do you think it is deeper than that? Support your argument by using the text.
- Why do you think the poet chooses to leave out a lot of the details about what happened?

Sister Maude has things in common with...
Death: To His Coy Mistress, p.6, Sonnet 43, p.10; Relationships: Brothers, p.28, Praise Song For My Mother, p.30; Negative Emotions: Nettles, p.14, Quickdraw, p.24.

Section One — Poems from the Literary Heritage

Vernon Scannell

Vernon Scannell (1922-2007) was born in Lincolnshire but moved frequently during his childhood. After a stint in the army, he became a professional boxer and then an English teacher. Many of his poems were shaped by his wartime experience.

Nettles

My son aged three fell in the nettle bed.
'Bed' seemed a curious name for those green spears,
That regiment of spite behind the shed:
It was no place for rest. With sobs and tears
5 The boy came seeking comfort and I saw
White blisters beaded on his tender skin.
We soothed him till his pain was not so raw.
At last he offered us a watery grin,
And then I took my hook and honed the blade
10 And went outside and slashed in fury with it
Till not a nettle in that fierce parade
Stood upright any more. Next task: I lit
A funeral pyre to burn the fallen dead.
But in two weeks the busy sun and rain
15 Had called up tall recruits behind the shed:
My son would often feel sharp wounds again.

Not all green spears are evil

POEM DICTIONARY
honed — sharpened

Nettles

Q1 Which of the emotions below are shown in this poem?
Find a quote to support each emotion you choose.

        anger   frustration   tenderness

Q2 a) Find three uses of military language in the poem.

    b) Why does the poet use military words?

Q3 How does Scannell try to get the reader to sympathise with his son?

Q4 Why do you think the story is told by a first person narrator?

Q5 Find an example of irony in this poem and explain why it is ironic.

Q6 This poem has a very simple rhyme scheme. Do you think this is appropriate, given the poem's subject matter? Explain your answer.

Q7 One of the themes of this poem is parents' helplessness at preventing their children from suffering. Why do you think the poet chose nettles as a symbol to explore this?

Extension activities
- Can you think of another metaphor that Scannell could have used instead of nettles that all readers would be able to understand?
- Write a short scene from a play based on the poem. Include dialogue from the father and his son.

Nettles shares themes with...
Negative Emotions: Harmonium, p.32, In Paris With You, p.22, Quickdraw, p.24; **Relationships:** Sister Maude, p.12, Praise Song For My Mother, p.30; **Getting Older:** Brothers, p.28.

Section One — Poems from the Literary Heritage

Philip Larkin

Philip Larkin (1922-1985) was born in Coventry. After graduating from Oxford he spent thirty years working as a librarian for the University of Hull, during which time he produced most of his great works of poetry. In 2008 he was named by The Times newspaper as England's best post-war writer.

Born Yesterday

for Sally Amis

Tightly-folded bud,
I have wished you something
None of the others would:
Not the usual stuff
5   About being beautiful,
Or running off a spring
Of innocence and love –
They will all wish you that,
And should it prove possible,
10   Well, you're a lucky girl.

But if it shouldn't, then
May you be ordinary;
Have, like other women,
An average of talents:
15   Not ugly, not good-looking,
Nothing uncustomary
To pull you off your balance,
That, unworkable itself,
Stops all the rest from working.
20   In fact, may you be dull –
If that is what a skilled,
Vigilant, flexible,
Unemphasised, enthralled
Catching of happiness is called.

"Look, when I said you were only a 5/10, it was a COMPLIMENT..."

Section One — Poems from the Literary Heritage

Born Yesterday

Q1   This poem was written for a newborn girl called Sally Amis.

   a)   What does Larkin wish for Sally in her life?

   b)   What does he suggest are the best ways for her to achieve this?

Q2   The poem does not contain many rhymes. What effect do you think this has?

Q3   What do you think is the importance of the poem's title?

Q4   In lines 21-23, Larkin uses five adjectives in quick succession. What effect do you think this has?

Q5   Choose a phrase from the poem which shows the narrator's viewpoint and say why it interests you.

Q6   In the first line of the poem, Larkin uses an image of a "tightly-folded bud" to describe newborn Sally. What impression does this give of how he sees her?

Extension activities
- How do you think you would feel if you were Sally Amis' parents hearing this poem?
- Do you agree with Larkin's view on the qualities that are needed for happiness? Give reasons for your answer.

Good poems to compare this to...
Getting Older: To His Coy Mistress, p.6, Brothers, p.28, Nettles, p.14; **Pain and Desire:** Sister Maude, p.12; **Love:** Sonnet 43, p.10, Praise Song For My Mother, p.30; **Nature:** Ghazal, p.26.

Section One — Poems from the Literary Heritage

Simon Armitage

Simon Armitage was born in 1963 in West Yorkshire. As well as poetry, he's also written four stage plays, and writes for TV, film and radio. He studied geography in Portsmouth, and he's now a Senior Lecturer in Creative Writing at Manchester Metropolitan University.

The Manhunt

After the first phase,
after passionate nights and intimate days,

only then would he let me trace
the frozen river which ran through his face,

5   only then would he let me explore
the blown hinge of his lower jaw,

and handle and hold
the damaged, porcelain collar-bone,

and mind and attend
10   the fractured rudder of shoulder-blade,

and finger and thumb
the parachute silk of his punctured lung.

Only then could I bind the struts
and climb the rungs of his broken ribs,

15   and feel the hurt
of his grazed heart.

Skirting along,
only then could I picture the scan,

the foetus of metal beneath his chest
20   where the bullet had finally come to rest.

Then I widened the search,
traced the scarring back to its source

to a sweating, unexploded mine
buried deep in his mind, around which

25   every nerve in his body had tightened and closed.
Then, and only then, did I come close.

The Manhunt

Q1 What do you think has happened to the person described in this poem?

Q2 Why do you think the poet chose 'The Manhunt' as the title of this poem?

Q3 Copy and complete the table below by choosing adjectives from the poem and saying why you think they are appropriate in this context.

Adjective	Effect
porcelain	It makes the soldier's body seem fragile and vulnerable.

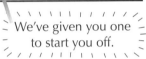
We've given you one to start you off.

Q4 Make a list of all the different emotions that you can identify in this poem. Give a quote which provides evidence for each one.

Q5 Do you think the narrator is claiming to understand what the soldier has been through? Back up your answer with quotes from the text.

Q6 Armitage has chosen to focus this poem on two individuals — the soldier and the narrator. What effect does this have on the way it allows us to see war?

Extension activity
- Do some research and see if you can find out why Armitage wrote this poem. Does this change your reaction to the poem? Why?

Poems which go well with The Manhunt...
Love: Nettles, p.14, Born Yesterday, p.16; **Relationships:** Praise Song For My Mother, p.30; **Negative Emotions:** Harmonium, p.32, Sister Maude, p.12; **Memory:** Brothers, p.28.

Section Two — Contemporary Poems

Carol Ann Duffy

Carol Ann Duffy was born in 1955 in Glasgow. She studied philosophy at the University of Liverpool, and in 1996 began lecturing in poetry at Manchester Metropolitan University. As well as writing poetry, she has also written plays. In 2009 she became the Poet Laureate.

Hour

Love's time's beggar, but even a single hour,
bright as a dropped coin, makes love rich.
We find an hour together, spend it not on flowers
or wine, but the whole of the summer sky and a grass ditch.

5   For thousands of seconds we kiss; your hair
like treasure on the ground; the Midas light
turning your limbs to gold. Time slows, for here
we are millionaires, backhanding the night

so nothing dark will end our shining hour,
10   no jewel hold a candle to the cuckoo spit
hung from the blade of grass at your ear,
no chandelier or spotlight see you better lit

than here. Now. Time hates love, wants love poor,
but love spins gold, gold, gold from straw.

POEM DICTIONARY
Midas — Mythical ancient Greek king who turned everything he touched into gold
cuckoo spit — white froth found on plants, produced by bugs

"I was made of flesh until I kissed Carol..."

Hour

Q1 If you didn't know that this poem was written by Carol Ann Duffy, what features would suggest that it's a modern poem?

Q2 Why do you think the poet chose to write this poem in sonnet form?

Q3 What is the effect of the enjambment in lines 5-6?

Q4 All the words in the final couplet of the poem have only one syllable.

   a) What is the effect of this?

   b) Does this fit in or contrast with the rest of the poem? How?

Q5 In the final couplet there's a reference to an old fairy tale — the story of Rumpelstiltskin. This fairy tale is the story of a dwarf who spins straw into gold.

   Why do you think the poet included this fairy tale image at the end of her poem?

Q6 In line 6, the poet refers to Midas. Midas was a Greek king who was granted the gift of being able to turn everything he touched into gold — but it turned out to be a curse rather than a gift.

   Why do you think this reference is included in the poem?

Extension activity

- This poem portrays love as being capable of slowing down time.
  Do you agree that love can sometimes feel this way? Give reasons for your answer.

Poems which have similar themes...
Love: In Paris With You, p.22, Sonnet 43, p.10; Relationships: To His Coy Mistress, p.6; Time: Sonnet 116, p.4; Nature: Ghazal, p.26, The Farmer's Bride, p.8, Praise Song, p.30.

Section Two — Contemporary Poems

James Fenton

James Fenton was born in 1949 in Lincoln. He studied at Magdalen College, Oxford, after which he travelled to East Asia and worked as a political journalist and war correspondent. In 2007 he was awarded the Queen's Gold Medal for Poetry.

In Paris With You

Don't talk to me of love. I've had an earful
And I get tearful when I've downed a drink or two.
I'm one of your talking wounded.
I'm a hostage. I'm maroonded.
5   But I'm in Paris with you.

Yes I'm angry at the way I've been bamboozled
And resentful at the mess I've been through.
I admit I'm on the rebound
And I don't care where are *we* bound.
10   I'm in Paris with you.

    Do you mind if we do *not* go to the Louvre,
    If we say sod off to sodding Notre Dame,
    If we skip the Champs Elysées
    And remain here in this sleazy
15   Old hotel room
    Doing this and that
    To what and whom
    Learning who you are,
    Learning what I am.

20   Don't talk to me of love. Let's talk of Paris,
The little bit of Paris in our view.
There's that crack across the ceiling
And the hotel walls are peeling
And I'm in Paris with you.

25   Don't talk to me of love. Let's talk of Paris.
I'm in Paris with the slightest thing you do.
I'm in Paris with your eyes, your mouth,
I'm in Paris with... all points south.
Am I embarrassing you?
30   I'm in Paris with you.

"Wait — that's not the
Eiffel tower!"

In Paris With You

Q1 Pick out two words or phrases from the poem which show the reader something about the poet's emotions.

Q2 Have a look at the copy of the poem on the left.
Which of the words below are used by Fenton to create a forced rhyme?

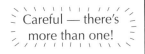

bamboozled   peeling   mouth   sleazy   maroonded

Q3 Fenton uses some unexpected adjectives to describe the landmarks of Paris.

   a) Find one example of this.

   b) What effect does it have on the poem as a whole?

Q4 Why do you think the poet asks "Am I embarrassing you?" in line 29?

Q5 This poem has a repeating stanza pattern, except for in the third stanza.

What effect does this have on the poem, and why do you think the poet chose to do it?

Q6 Some readers might describe the narrator of this poem as self-pitying.

To what extent do you agree with this view?
Back up your answer with quotes from the poem.

Extension activity
- The poem gives us no details of the poet's companion's feelings, except for one brief hint at the end. Write a postcard from this person to a friend, giving their feelings on their stay in Paris.

More like this...
Relationships: To His Coy Mistress, p.6, Hour, p.20, Sonnet 116, p.4; **Negative Emotions:** Sister Maude, p.12, Harmonium, p.32, Quickdraw, p.24; **Pain and Desire:** The Farmer's Bride, p.8.

Section Two — Contemporary Poems

Carol Ann Duffy

Carol Ann Duffy was born in 1955 in Glasgow. She studied philosophy at the University of Liverpool, and in 1996 began lecturing in poetry at Manchester Metropolitan University. As well as writing poetry, she has also written plays. In 2009 she became the Poet Laureate.

Quickdraw

I wear the two, the mobile and the landline phones,
like guns, slung from the pockets on my hips. I'm all
alone. You ring, quickdraw, your voice a pellet
in my ear, and hear me groan.

5   You've wounded me.
Next time, you speak after the tone. I twirl the phone,
then squeeze the trigger of my tongue, wide of the mark.
You choose your spot, then blast me

                                                               through the heart.
10 And this is love, high noon, calamity, hard liquor
in the old Last Chance saloon. I show the mobile
to the Sheriff; in my boot, another one's

concealed. You text them both at once. I reel.
Down on my knees, I fumble for the phone,
15 read the silver bullets of your kiss. Take this ...
and this ... and this ... and this ... and this ...

Quickdraw

Q1 In this poem, what is the effect of:

a) the differing line lengths?

b) the use of enjambment?

"Honestly Officer, I don't have any credit."

Q2 Duffy uses Western films as an analogy in this poem. Find three examples of words or phrases in the poem which are part of this analogy.

Q3 Western films are now often considered outdated.

What effect does the use of language about Westerns have?
How does this combine with the phone technology mentioned in the poem?

Q4 Choose an image from the poem which you think is especially effective and explain why you chose it.

Q5 Duffy refers to the person on the other end of the phone as "the Sheriff". Why do you think this might be?

Q6 Do you empathise with the narrator of the poem? Why/why not?

Extension activities
- In line 8, the narrator says, "You choose your spot, then blast me". What do you think the person on the other end of the phone might have said?
- Do you think the Western analogy is successful? Explain the reasons for your answer.

Compare and contrast this poem with...
<u>Negative Emotions</u>: Sister Maude, p.12, In Paris With You, p.22; <u>Pain and Desire</u>: Nettles, p.14, To His Coy Mistress, p.6; <u>Relationships</u>: Brothers, p.28; <u>Love</u>: Ghazal, p.26, The Manhunt, p18.

Section Two — Contemporary Poems

Mimi Khalvati

<u>Mimi Khalvati</u> was born in 1944 in Tehran. She went to boarding school on the Isle of Wight, then studied in London. She founded The Poetry School, where she is now a tutor, and has worked as an actor and director in the UK and Iran.

Ghazal

If I am the grass and you the breeze, blow through me.
If I am the rose and you the bird, then woo me.

If you are the rhyme and I the refrain, don't hang
on my lips, come and I'll come too when you cue me.

5   If yours is the iron fist in the velvet glove
when the arrow flies, the heart is pierced, tattoo me.

If mine is the venomous tongue, the serpent's tail,
charmer, use your charm, weave a spell and subdue me.

If I am the laurel leaf in your crown, you are
10   the arms around my bark, arms that never knew me.

Oh would that I were bark! So old and still in leaf.
And you, dropping in my shade, dew to bedew me!

What shape should I take to marry your own, have you
– hawk to my shadow, moth to my flame – pursue me?

15   If I rise in the east as you die in the west,
die for my sake, my love, every night renew me.

If, when it ends, we are just good friends, be my Friend,
muse, lover and guide, Shamsuddin to my Rumi.

Be heaven and earth to me and I'll be twice the me
20   I am, if only half the world you are to me.

<u>POEM DICTIONARY</u>
refrain — a line that is repeated in poetry or song
laurel — laurel leaves in a wreath are traditional symbols of victory
bedew — make something wet — like dew
muse — someone who inspires an artist
Shamsuddin — or Shams Tabrizi, the mystical friend and mentor of the poet Rumi
Rumi — important religious figure and poet. He was close friends with Shams (or Shamsuddin)
— when Shams disappeared Rumi was inspired to write mystical poetry.

Ghazal

Q1 A ghazal is a poem that uses a strict couplet form to express the beauty of love, the pain that love can bring and the triumph of love over that pain.

   a)   Find a line or phrase in the poem that supports each of the three themes above.

   b)   What effect do you think the couplet form has?

Q2 What do you think is meant by "I rise in the east as you die in the west" (line 15)?

Q3 How does the narrator compare herself to her lover? What effect does this have?

Q4 Why do you think the poet uses so much natural imagery in this ghazal?

Q5 What title would you give this ghazal? Give reasons for your answer.

Q6 Do you think this is a positive or negative poem overall? Support your answer by referring to the text.

Extension activities
- Shamsuddin and Rumi were real people. Find out who they were and what happened to them. Does this knowledge help you to understand the ghazal better than before?
- Do you think the poem tells you anything about what the narrator's lover is like?

Poems which talk about the same feelings...
<u>Love</u>: Sonnet 43, p.10, Sonnet 116, p.4, Quickdraw, p.24; <u>Relationships</u>: Nettles, p.18, The Manhunt, p.18; <u>Nature</u>: Praise Song For My Mother, p.30, Hour, p.20, The Farmer's Bride, p.8.

Section Two — Contemporary Poems

Andrew Forster

Andrew Forster was born in South Yorkshire. His first poetry collection, 'Fear of Thunder', was published in 2007.

Brothers

Saddled with you for the afternoon, me and Paul
ambled across the threadbare field to the bus stop,
talking over Sheffield Wednesday's chances in the Cup
while you skipped beside us in your ridiculous tank-top,
5   spouting six-year-old views on Rotherham United.

Suddenly you froze, said you hadn't any bus fare.
I sighed, said you should go and ask Mum
and while you windmilled home I looked at Paul.
His smile, like mine, said I was nine and he was ten
10 and we must stroll the town, doing what grown-ups do.

As a bus crested the hill we chased Olympic Gold.
Looking back I saw you spring towards the gate,
your hand holding out what must have been a coin.
I ran on, unable to close the distance I'd set in motion.

"I was nine and he was ten, why not scribble
all over us with thick, black pen..."

Section Two — Contemporary Poems

Brothers

Q1 From the choices below, identify the three main feelings talked about in this poem.

pride   frustration   guilt   regret   joy

Q2 Find a phrase or line from the poem that shows:

a) that the boys think they are mature
b) that they are actually quite child-like

Q3 What is the effect of the contrast between childishness and maturity?

Q4 What evidence can you find that this poem was written in hindsight?

Q5 What does the final stanza suggest about the narrator's overriding feelings?

Q6 What do you think is the importance of the metaphor "we chased Olympic Gold"?

Extension activity
- Imagine you are the younger brother in this poem. Write a short letter to the narrator explaining how you felt about the event at the time and how you feel about it now.

Poems which touch on the same issues...
Relationships: Sister Maude, p.12, Nettles, p.14; Negative Emotions: The Manhunt, p.18, In Paris With You, p.22, The Farmer's Bride, p.8; Getting Older: Praise Song For My Mother, p.30.

Section Two — Contemporary Poems

Grace Nichols

Grace Nichols was born in Guyana in 1950. She was a teacher and journalist in the Caribbean until she moved to Britain in 1977. Both of these cultures and how they interlink are important to her.

Praise Song For My Mother

You were
water to me
deep and bold and fathoming

You were
5   moon's eye to me
pull and grained and mantling

You were
sunrise to me
rise and warm and streaming

10   You were
the fish's red gill to me
the flame tree's spread to me
the crab's leg/the fried plantain smell
                replenishing replenishing

15   Go to your wide futures, you said

You were
the freakiest photo I have ever seen

POEM DICTIONARY
fathoming — getting to the bottom of something, or measuring the depth of something
grained — textured like the surface of wood
mantling — covering or wrapping up — a mantle is a type of cloak
plantain — a banana-like food from the Caribbean

Praise Song For My Mother

Q1 a) What does the title of this poem lead you to expect?

   b) Is your expectation fulfilled by the poem?

Q2 At the end of the poem, Nichols' mother does a very important thing for her. What does this suggest about her character?

Q3 What evidence can you find for the influence of Caribbean culture on the poem?

Q4 How does the poet's use of fairly simple language support the theme of the poem?

Q5 What effect do the words which have double meanings, e.g. "mantling", "streaming", "fathoming", have on the poem?

Q6 What impression do you think the mother's words at the end of the poem give? Refer back to earlier parts of the poem to support your answer.

Extension activities
- What four images would you use to describe someone you love in place of the ones Nichols uses in lines 10-13?
- Do you think the poem would lose some of its impact if it was written in sonnet form?

Poems in a similar vein...
Love: Nettles, p.14, The Manhunt, p.18, Sonnet 43, p.10, Sonnet 116, p.4; Time: Hour, p.20, To His Coy Mistress, p.6; Getting Older: Brothers, p.28, Born Yesterday, p.16, Harmonium, p.32.

Section Two — Contemporary Poems

Simon Armitage

Simon Armitage was born in 1963 in West Yorkshire. As well as poetry, he's also written four stage plays, and writes for TV, film and radio. He studied geography in Portsmouth, and he's now a Senior Lecturer in Creative Writing at Manchester Metropolitan University.

Harmonium

The *Farrand Chapelette* was gathering dust
in the shadowy porch of Marsden Church.
And was due to be bundled off to the skip.
Or was mine, for a song, if I wanted it.

5   Sunlight, through stained glass, which day to day
could beatify saints and raise the dead,
had aged the harmonium's softwood case
and yellowed the fingernails of its keys.
And one of its notes had lost its tongue,
10   and holes were worn in both the treadles
where the organist's feet, in grey, woollen socks
and leather-soled shoes, had pedalled and pedalled.

But its hummed harmonics still struck a chord:
for a hundred years that organ had stood
15   by the choristers' stalls, where father and son,
each in their time, had opened their throats
and gilded finches – like high notes – had streamed out.

Through his own blue cloud of tobacco smog,
with smoker's fingers and dottled thumbs,
20   he comes to help me cart it away.
And we carry it flat, laid on its back.
And he, being him, can't help but say
that the next box I'll shoulder through this nave
will bear the freight of his own dead weight.
25   And I, being me, then mouth in reply
some shallow or sorry phrase or word
too starved of breath to make itself heard.

POEM DICTIONARY
harmonium — a type of organ which was often found in small churches, operated by pumping two treadles
Marsden — a village in West Yorkshire
beatify — declare someone's holiness or make very happy
treadle — a lever you work with your foot
gilded — covered with a layer of gold
dottled — tobacco stained

Section Two — Contemporary Poems

Harmonium

Q1   Using the poem as a guide, write a description of the harmonium.

"I don't know what you're smiling at — you'll be carrying me soon enough"

Q2   Give one example of humorous language in this poem.

Q3   Why do you think Armitage uses so many half-rhymes in this poem,
e.g. "And was due to be bundled off to the skip. / Or was mine, for a song, if I wanted it."?

Q4   Copy and complete the table below by choosing images from
the poem and saying why you think they are effective.

Image	Effective because...
blue cloud of tobacco smog (line 18)	"blue cloud" is quite beautiful, so it provides a strong contrast with the idea of "tobacco smog".

We've given you one to start you off.

Q5   How would you describe the tone in the last stanza of the poem?

Extension activities
- Try to write your own description of a special musical instrument, for example an antique violin or a worn-out piano.
- What impression do you get of the poet's father from this poem?

If you like this, you'll like...
<u>Negative Emotions</u>: The Manhunt, p.18, The Farmer's Bride, p.8; <u>Death</u>: Sister Maude, p.12, Sonnet 43, p.10; <u>Relationships</u>: Praise Song For My Mother, p.30, Brothers, p.28.

Section Two — Contemporary Poems

Relationships

Q1 a) Write a list of five different types of relationship.

b) For each type, think of something that can cause a problem with the relationship.

c) Which do you think is the strongest kind of relationship and why?

Q2 Choose a poem from the cluster that describes a relationship and make notes on the following:

a) Does the poet present a positive or negative impression of the relationship? Explain your answer.

b) Are there any similarities between this relationship and a relationship involving you or someone you know?

Q3 Choose a different poem.

a) Which of these words describes the poet's feelings about the person or people in the relationship described in the poem?

respect	hatred	anger	love
tenderness	sympathy	disgust	disillusionment
guilt	lust	frustration	humour

b) Choose three words of your own to describe the poet's feelings. Find a quote from the poem to support each one.

c) Are there any contradictions between the feelings about relationships in this poem, or are the feelings consistent? Can you explain why this is?

Section Three — Themes

Relationships

Q4 Choose two different poems that deal with relationships.
Copy out the table below and fill it in with notes about the poems.

	Poem 1	Poem 2
Form		
Structure		
Type of relationship described		
Imagery used		

Q5 Look again at the two poems you chose for Q4.

a) Which of the poems presents a more positive image of the relationship? Use a quote from each poem to support your point.

b) Do you agree with the way the characters in the poems deal with the issues in their relationships?

c) How can you explain the differences in the two poets' attitudes to relationships?

Exam-Style Questions

Remember to make a proper plan before you start writing out your answer.

06 Compare how relationships are presented in *To His Coy Mistress* and **one** other poem from 'Relationships'. *(36 marks)*

07 Compare how feelings are shown in *Ghazal* and **one** other poem from 'Relationships'. *(36 marks)*

Section Three — Themes

Negative Emotions

Q1 Think about a time when you have had very negative emotions. Write a short description of how you felt.

"My middle name is NOT 'Negative'", said Rachael. "It's 'Cynical'..."

Q2 Below is a list of poems from the Relationships cluster. Pick out the ones which talk about anger.

Hour	In Paris With You	The Manhunt
Sister Maude	Ghazal	Harmonium
Sonnet 116	Nettles	The Farmer's Bride

Q3 For each of the emotions below, choose a poem which portrays that emotion and then provide a quote from the poem which provides evidence for that emotion.

   a) guilt

   b) bitterness

Q4 Look again at the poems that you chose for Q2.
How is language used in these poems to present negative emotions?

Q5 Now pick another poem from the cluster that talks about a negative emotion.
Explain how the poet's choice of form helps to convey that emotion.

Section Three — Themes

Love

Q1 "All the poems in the Relationships cluster talk about romantic love." Do you agree?

Q2 From the poetry cluster choose a poem which uses each of the following to describe love:

   a) A metaphor   b) Personification

Q3 Some love is selfless — it asks for nothing in return. Make a list of poems which present this kind of love and find a quote for each that supports this idea.

Q4 Choose one of the poems that you picked for Q3 and explain how the poet presents love as selfless. Try to comment on the poem's language and structure in your answer.

Q5 What theme do the poems 'In Paris With You', 'The Farmer's Bride' and 'Sonnet 43' have in common?

Q6 Do you think the poems in this cluster present love as a positive or negative emotion overall? Support your answer with reference to at least two poems.

Exam-Style Questions

07 Compare how negative emotions are presented in *Harmonium* and **one** other poem from 'Relationships'. *(36 marks)*

08 Compare how poets use language to express love in *Nettles* and **one** other poem from 'Relationships'. *(36 marks)*

Section Three — Themes

Time

Q1 Each of the following lines of poetry personifies time. For each one, say which poem it is taken from.

   a) "Time hates love, wants love poor"
   b) "Love's not Time's fool, though rosy lips and cheeks"
   c) "Time's wingèd chariot hurrying near"

Q2 Create a table like the one below to show how two of the poems in the anthology use language, structure and form to present the theme of time.

Poem	Language to present time	Structure/form to present time

Q3 Find quotes from two different poems which support the idea that time spent together is precious.

Q4 Choose a poem from the 'Literary Heritage' section which uses time as a theme. How does the poet use time in this poem?

Q5 Now choose a poem from the 'Contemporary Poems' section. What ideas does the poet present about time?

Q6 Pick one poem from the 'Literary Heritage' section of the anthology, and one from the 'Contemporary Poems' section.

Do you think that the contemporary poem portrays the relationship between love and time differently to the literary heritage poem? How?

Section Three — Themes

Getting Older

Q1 Say whether each of the statements below is true or false.
Find a quote from the poem to support or disagree with each statement.

- In *Brothers* the narrator thinks he behaved like a grown-up when he was nine.

- Larkin thinks it's a good thing to grow up to be nothing special.

- In *Harmonium* Armitage is uncomfortable around his ageing father.

- Age is one of the things that causes a problem in *The Farmer's Bride*.

- In *Sonnet 116* Shakespeare portrays love as something which fades with age.

Q2 Choose a poem from the 'Literary Heritage' section of the anthology.
How does the character in the poem feel about getting older?

Q3 Choose a poem from the 'Contemporary Poems' section of the anthology which explores the theme of getting older.

a) What is the attitude to ageing in this poem?

b) How is this attitude conveyed?

Q4 Choose a poem where you empathise with the view of ageing. Explain why you empathise with it, using quotes from the poem to back up your answer.

Exam-Style Questions

0 5 "Time is one of the few things we cannot change, no matter how hard we try."
Compare how *Hour* and **one** other poem from 'Relationships' present the inevitability of time. *(36 marks)*

0 6 Compare how the theme of getting older is approached in
Praise Song For My Mother and **one** other poem from 'Relationships'. *(36 marks)*

Section Three — Themes

Death

Q1   "All the poems in the anthology portray death in a negative way." Do you agree?

Q2   Link the poem titles below with the aspect of death that they talk about.

Harmonium	Wishing for someone's death
Sonnet 43	Love surviving beyond death
To His Coy Mistress	Difficulty talking about death
Sister Maude	Death is motivation for enjoying life
Sonnet 116	Love becoming stronger after death

Q3   Most people find death a difficult subject to talk about. Bearing this in mind, why do you think many of the anthology poets choose to include death as a theme in their work?

Q4   Choose a poem from the anthology that has death as one of its themes.
Look at the language that the poet has used to talk about death.

Is there anything about their choice of language that surprises you? Explain your answer.

Q5   *Sonnet 43*, *Sonnet 116* and *Harmonium* are all poems which talk about death. Which of these poems do you find most moving? Explain your answer.

Q6   Some people might argue that *In Paris With You* is a poem about the death of a relationship. To what extent do you agree with this? Support your answer by referring to the poem.

Section Three — Themes

Memory

Q1 Write down the names of four poems that have memory as a theme. Now draw a spider diagram and see if you can list all the memories they talk about without looking back at the poems.

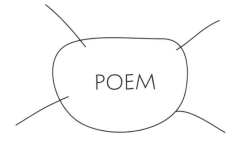

"YOU FORGOT THE CRAB'S LEGS!"

Q2 Choose a poem which presents positive memories. What language is used to make them sound positive?

Q3 Poets often include sensory details when talking about their memories. Read over the poems that you picked for Q1, and write down three different sensory details.

e.g. sound, sight, smell, taste or touch

Q4 Do you think there are any similarities in the tone that *The Farmer's Bride* and *Brothers* use when dealing with the theme of memory?

Q5 Which poem do you think is most successful at communicating its ideas about memory, and why?

Exam-Style Questions

| 0 | 6 | Compare how death is presented in *Harmonium* and **one** other poem from 'Relationships'. *(36 marks)*

| 0 | 7 | Compare how *The Manhunt* and **one** other poem from 'Relationships' use memory to explore their message. *(36 marks)*

Section Three — Themes

Nature

Q1 Why do you think poets choose to include images of nature in their poems?

Q2 Link the images of nature below with the poem they come from.

hawk to my shadow, moth to my flame	*Praise Song For My Mother*
Sweet as the first wild violets, she	*The Farmer's Bride*
hung from the blade of grass at your ear	*To His Coy Mistress*
And now, like amorous birds of prey,	*Hour*
the flame tree's spread to me	*Ghazal*

Q3 Choose a poem from the 'Literary Heritage' section.

a) What aspect of nature does the poet describe?

b) What does this add to the thoughts, feelings or attitudes in the poem?

Q4 Now choose a poem from the 'Contemporary Poems' section. How is nature used in this poem?

Q5 Nature can be presented as either a positive or negative force.

Create a table like the one below and list all of the poems which refer to nature. Say whether they present nature as a good or bad force and give a quote from the poem that backs this up.

Poem	Nature — good or bad?	Quote

Q6 'Nettles' is the only poem in the cluster which refers to nature in its title.

Do you think it presents nature differently to the other poems? Explain your answer using quotes from 'Nettles' and at least one other poem.

Section Three — Themes

Pain and Desire

Q1 Find a poem in the anthology where someone is:

   a) physically hurt

   b) emotionally hurt

Q2 Choose a poem where a character wishes for something they can't have.

   a) What are they wishing for?

   b) How do they express this desire?

Q3 The characters in the anthology poems often become frustrated because they cannot fulfil their desires.
Use a thesaurus to look up words connected to frustration, then try to say which of the poems they apply to.

"Hello — I've been a very naughty boy..."

Q4 Pick a poem that talks about pain. Does the form support the theme? Explain your answer.

Q5 Pick another poem that talks about pain. Do you feel sympathy for the character in the poem? Why/why not?

Exam-Style Questions

| 0 | 6 | Compare *To His Coy Mistress* and **one** other poem from 'Relationships' and say why you find their use of nature particularly effective.   *(36 marks)*

| 0 | 7 | Compare how desire is presented in *The Farmer's Bride* and **one** other poem from 'Relationships'.   *(36 marks)*

Section Three — Themes

Mark Scheme

This section is a bit different — it's your chance to get inside the examiner's mind.

1) The mark scheme below is very similar to the one that the examiners will use to mark your actual exam answers.

2) The point of this section is to show you exactly what the examiners are looking for and what you'll need to do on the day to get high marks.

3) You have to read the sample extracts of exam answers. Then you'll either mark the answer and say how it can be improved, or add some extra points to make the answer better. The mark scheme will help you do this.

4) Before you start grading the sample answers, make sure you've read the mark scheme really thoroughly and that you understand everything.

Grade	What you've written
A*	• Explores several interpretations or meanings in detail • Provides carefully chosen and well-integrated quotes to back up ideas • Compares the poems thoughtfully and in detail, using plenty of evidence • Looks closely at how language, form and structure affect the reader, with well-chosen examples • Gives detailed and imaginative ideas about themes, attitudes and feelings • Considers the evidence to come up with conclusions about the poem
A	• Gives several interpretations or meanings • Provides well-chosen quotes to support ideas • Compares the poems in detail and provides plenty of evidence • Describes how language, form and structure affect the reader, using examples • Looks at themes, attitudes and feelings in detail, again using plenty of evidence
B	• Thoughtful interpretation of the poems • Supports interpretations with quotes from the text • Provides some well-chosen evidence to support comparisons between the poems • Gives several examples of how language, form and structure affect the reader • Provides some evidence to support ideas about themes, attitudes and feelings
C	• Comments on several aspects of the poem, e.g. mood, language, feelings, and uses quotes to back the comments up • Makes several comparisons between the poems • Explains how language, form and structure affect the reader • Makes valid comments about themes, attitudes or feelings in the poems

You'll also be marked on your spelling, punctuation and grammar and on how you present your work. To get the best marks, your essay should be clearly organised into well-structured paragraphs. It should also be easy to follow and understand.

Adding Quotes and Developing Points

The sample answers on this page have just one thing missing. Your task is to improve each point by adding a quote from the poem which backs it up. Good luck...

> **0 1** Compare how poets present ideas about relationships in
> *To His Coy Mistress* and one other poem from 'Relationships'. *(36 marks)*

Answer Extract 1

In this sample answer, some sentences have letters like this: **(A)**.
Replace each letter with a suitable quote to help the student get a better grade.

> In 'To His Coy Mistress' and 'In Paris With You', the poets both use different types of language to show relationships between men and women. In 'To His Coy Mistress', Marvell writes about the effect that being in love has on people. He uses exaggeration, such as **(A)**, to show that people in love will do extreme things for the people that they care about. On the other hand, Fenton has a more negative view about the way in which people treat one another in relationships, saying **(B)**.
>
> Neither of the poems seems to really be about love; they are more about lust. The first poem speaks of love, for example, "I would / Love you", but he doesn't claim to actually love her. In the second poem, the poet uses negative language such as **(C)**, to show how the idea of love makes him feel.

Answer Extract 2

In this sample answer, some sentences have letters like this: **(A)**.
Replace each letter with a suitable quote to help the student get a better grade.

> The poets of both 'To His Coy Mistress' and 'In Paris With You' make use of language to present their ideas about relationships effectively. In both poems, the theme appears to be love, but on closer reading, it is quite clear that they are really about lust.
>
> In the first poem, the use of the word "coy" in the title suggests that the woman that the poet is speaking to is both shy and flirtatious. He shows that he has strong feelings for her when he uses exaggerated language, such as **(A)**, to talk about her and their relationship. On the other hand, Fenton is clear that his feelings are far from strong, as we can tell from the way he says **(B)**.

Section Four — Analysing Answers

Adding Quotes and Developing Points

Two more extracts and two more tasks on this page — develop the points and finish the plan.

> **0 1** Compare how poets present ideas about relationships in
> *To His Coy Mistress* and one other poem from 'Relationships'. *(36 marks)*

Answer Extract 3

In this sample answer, some sentences have letters like this: **(A)**. These points need to be developed further. Write an extra sentence to develop each point.

> Both 'To His Coy Mistress' and 'In Paris With You' use language to show ideas about love and lust. In the first poem, Marvell uses the word "love" four times, which might suggest that he is writing a love poem to his mistress. However, whenever he mentions love, he does so in the future tense, which seems to suggest that he does not love her at present. In the second poem, the word "love" is always used negatively when Fenton writes "Don't talk to me of love."
>
> In both poems, the idea of lust seems more important than the idea of love. Both poets talk euphemistically about sex, with Marvell suggesting that they "sport us while we may" and Fenton that they "remain here in this sleazy / Old hotel room". **(A)** In 'In Paris With You', the use of the word "you" seems to be ambiguous. Unlike Marvell, Fenton is not writing for a specific person; rather he seems to be writing for the person that he is with at the time. **(B)** This supports the idea that the poem is about sex, not love, because there seems only to be a physical relationship between them.

> **0 2** Compare the ways in which ideas about relationships are presented
> in *Sonnet 116* and one other poem in 'Relationships'. *(36 marks)*

Sample Plan

The table below is a plan for an answer to the question above.

Find a quotation from the poem to back up each of the language points in the table.
Make brief notes on your personal response to each poem to complete the plan.

	Sonnet 116	**Hour**
Themes and ideas	Argues that true love never changes	Says time is precious when you're in love
Language	Of sailing; a journey ... **(A)** Of time ... **(B)**	Of time ... **(C)** Of money and wealth ... **(D)**
Form and Structure	Sonnet – is a love poem. The turn lines – proof that he's telling the truth	Sonnet – is a love poem
Personal Response	**(E)**	**(F)**

Section Four — Analysing Answers

Marking Answer Extracts

This page is all about marking sample exam answers. If you're reading this without having read the mark scheme on p.44 first — do not collect £200 and certainly DO NOT pass GO.

> **0 3** Compare how feelings towards another person are presented in *Nettles* and one other poem from 'Relationships'. *(36 marks)*

Answer Extract 4

1) Use the mark scheme to <u>mark</u> this extract.
2) <u>Explain</u> how you decided on the grade and say how the answer could be <u>improved</u>.

This first extract has been marked for you to show you what to do.

> 'Nettles' presents feelings towards family members as unambiguous and uncomplicated, because it uses a simple narrative form and precise images, such as "White blisters beaded on his tender skin", to make it easily understandable to the reader.
> However, 'In Paris With You' suggests feelings towards lovers are more complicated. Fenton seems angry with his previous partner, who has "bamboozled" him, but his unwillingness to get closer to his current lover suggests he was badly hurt and is not going to let it happen again. The form reinforces the feelings of anger when it repeats "Don't" at the beginning of most stanzas.

Response: This answer gets a grade **B** because it talks about the themes of the poems and how the language, structure and form affect the reader, and provides examples of these things. However, it has only provided one possible interpretation of the poems, which prevents it from being a grade A.

Answer Extract 5

1) Use the mark scheme to <u>mark</u> this extract from a sample answer to the question above.
2) <u>Explain</u> how you decided on the grade and say how the answer could be <u>improved</u>.

> 'Nettles' is about the relationship between a father and his son, whilst 'Born Yesterday' is written as a wish for someone else's child. Both poems show how the poets feel about the different children.
> In 'Nettles', the poet describes his feelings for his young son. He talks about the day that his son hurt himself: "fell in the nettle bed". He describes how he "soothed" his son, which suggests that he took time and care to make him feel better; something which clearly shows how much he loves and cares for the boy. This is an ordinary thing for a parent to do when a child is hurt, which is similar to 'Born Yesterday', where Larkin shows how much he cares for Sally Amis. He says he wants her to have "An average of talents". This shows that he knows that being "ordinary" is actually a good thing, and something worth celebrating.

Section Four — Analysing Answers

Marking Answer Extracts

Here's the exam question again and an extract from a sample answer to it.

> **0 3** Compare how feelings towards another person are presented in *Nettles* and one other poem from 'Relationships'. *(36 marks)*

Answer Extract 6

1) Use the mark scheme on p.44 to <u>mark</u> this extract.
2) <u>Explain</u> how you decided on the grade and say how the answer could be <u>improved</u>.

Both 'Nettles' and 'Born Yesterday' are about the ordinary feelings that the poets have for the person that they are writing for. In 'Nettles', the poet is writing about the love and fear he has for his own son, whilst Larkin is writing about the ordinary things that he hopes for for Sally Amis, his friend's daughter.

'Nettles' opens with a fairly ordinary event from everyone's childhood, falling "in the nettle bed", and a father's ordinary response to it: he "soothed him till his pain was not so raw." The reader can recognise this from their own childhood, and see how ordinary the soothing is, as well as how this shows the father's love. We know that the father cannot actually make the pain go away, but the fact that the child goes to his father "seeking comfort" shows that he knows that he is loved. In 'Born Yesterday', Larkin describes how other people wish fairy-tale things like "being beautiful" on the newborn baby, but how he wishes ordinary things such as "An average of talents" on her. This, like 'Nettles', shows that he cares for the child because he is only concerned with what will make her happy.

Scannell's love for his son is not only shown through the care that he shows him, but also in the way he goes on to deal with the cause of his pain. Even though the child soon recovers from his accident, the poet is angry about the hurt that has been caused, and destroys the nettles in an attempt to protect him from future hurt. The description of him as he "slashed in fury" shows how his love means that he wants to hurt the nettles like they hurt his son.

Keep looking back at the mark scheme so you know exactly what you should be looking for — don't just think "Oh, it's not bad, I'll give it a C."

Section Four — Analysing Answers